Be a Giver of Awesomeness

DISCOVER | GUARD | GIVE

Raushawna Price

Your Mindset and Perspective Will Be Enlightened!

"Working with Raushawna as my leadership coach for 6 weeks allowed me to push myself to change my mindset and think about how I interacted with my team and network in a whole new way. She has an uncanny ability to ask the right questions which led to breakthroughs in my thinking...I highly recommend investing in your future by working with Raushawna. Your mindset and perspective will be enlightened!"...Emily S.

She Leads With Passion

"Raushawna is an inspirational leader who understands that successful leaders are those who serve. She leads with this passion and is committed to helping others develop to their fullest potential."...Ruth S.

I Was Broken...and She Showed Me How Whole I Was "

"During our leadership training we did an affirmation activity. The activity helped me see that people see me better than I see myself. To know that someone values me in every category was truly uplifting. To know someone actually trusts me, WOW!!! I thank God for them and the training."...F. O'Neal

Extremely Helpful and Enlightening

"Working with Raushawna was extremely helpful and enlightening for both my personal and professional life. Her listening skills are incredible and her insight into behaviors was logical and well thought out...I would recommend her to anyone needing coaching for any part of their life."...Susan S.

Dedication

To my Mom, thank you for answering the phone and funding the beginning of my crazy.

To Jovani, my greatest love, thank you for telling me I'm not crazy when it sure felt like I was.

Karen,
You are beautiful!
I love your personality +
pray this book shows
you _more_ of your Awesomeness.

This is Your year of GROWTH!

♡
Roshawn

Table of Contents

Part I - Discover

When bullies come, you know you have a gift.

Chapter 1 – The Catalyst

Sometimes a pothole in the road can cause a flat tire.

I AM GOING through the journey of life, on my way, happy, healthy, loved, and then BOOM, my "I didn't sign up for this" moment happened. My "how did I get here" moment came barreling at me like a heavyweight boxer uppercut. It landed with a fierce blow that left my ears ringing, and my eyes blurry. The physical evidence of the blow is not always distinguishable to the eye, however, the spiritual and emotional wounds cut deep and take time to heal.

I was sitting in a bathroom stall in a hotel lobby crying my eyes out the last time I had one of those moments. That moment lead me here, to you. It was in the bathroom stall, talking to God asking him to help me remember this moment and learn from it that changed me. I needed clarity, courage, and fixing. My heart was broken, therefore, I was broken.

I had been working on a project and I thought my effort was good enough. I thought I understood the landscape and topography to navigate this complex project when the truth was, I was unaware of the landmines of the spirit and heart I was facing. In the restroom is where I found courage and power to guard my gifts and talents, my Awesomeness. It is in the restroom where I decided to begin thinking and reshaping what I wanted and what I felt God was calling me to do.

> I asked God,
> How did I get here?

I was in a quiet place and it was safe and small. I needed to feel safe. I felt mini inside, and all I wanted was to fit into the expectation of someone else. It is also in that stall that I found I had been in this place in my life before. I cried. I wrote in my journal and I asked God, "how did I get here?". I also watched a couple superhero movie clips (I love superheros)! I had to do something to get my courage up to be able to come out of the stall and keep going. Also, I believed the moment was significant and I wanted to know why. The lessons I learned would be uncovered over the course of the next several months. I explored patterns in my life and the outcome of this inner work is written in this book. I wrote it to free myself and perhaps free you, too.

I figured out I had been in this place before. A place of sadness and hurt, feeling uncertain because of words that cut me to my core. Words that did not match the behavior that I exhibited but were used against me as weapons to inflict pain and diminish my ability to persist.

I realized that people, when hurt, can feel small, insignificant, and out of control. I also noticed that a hurt woman in power is dangerous. Women in "power" hurt other women when they forget or refuse to place limits on what they will and won't say. When they say what they feel without carefully measuring the reverberated consequences of their words on the lives of others. Emptiness is what happens when our lives collide into a woman who means well but does MEAN, well.

I believe these women and situations are gifts and messages from God. This may not be your belief and that is okay. No matter what you believe, I believe this book can help you find your inner Awesomeness. It is in there and it is ready to come out.

My hope for you as you read this book is that you will journey within to find your secret place where you will find your dreams and passions that have been waiting for you! I hope you will bring them out. When you do your gifts, your talents, and what I call Awesomeness is what the world needs.

Beyond hope, this books offers questions to help you prepare for what is next. I often tell my clients "hope is not a strategy." Use the resources in this book to build a strategy that

> Be bold in your thinking and intentional in your answers.

you can execute. Be bold in your thinking and intentional in your answers. When you get to a question that is hard, that is where treasure awaits. Don't skip it. Ponder the question and be courageous to let your real answer come out. Find it, claim it, and use it to propel you forward towards who you are really meant to be.

Chapter 2 –The Bullying Begin

You sound like a white girl.

I QUICKLY LEARNED that I was different in elementary school. In a small town in upstate New York, as a fourth grader, learning how to play the trumpet, getting decent grades and dancing (tap, ballet, jazz, and modern), I was doing **my** thing. Then, "Raushawna's the white girl." Yes, "white girl" would be the words yelled out to me, posted outside my locker and passed to me on white pieces of paper in secret. My first bullying experience.

At first, it was mocking and name calling. I got to a point when I didn't like speaking in public. In fourth grade, I was asked to read a paragraph out loud in front of the class. I was so nervous. I hated reading out loud. I didn't want people to whisper about my voice, the way I talked and sounded. I got so nervous. I lied. Right there sitting at my desk, I told my teacher I couldn't see the words on the page. I faked it. I said I could not see and that perhaps I was getting sick and needed to go to the eye doctor. I started crying at my desk, got so upset that I was sent out of the classroom and to the nurse's office. It's funny now, but I remember my Mom even took me to the eye doctor where they found my eye sight to be fine (of course) and they diagnosed me with having a "panic attack" of sorts. Yup, that was me all right, panicked about being picked on!

The mocking and being picked on escalated and by the time I was in the sixth grade, I was booed while walking through the cafeteria on my way to the library. I did not want to go to the library and I definitely didn't want to walk by myself. I took a deep breath before pulling open the door to the

> The shame was the worst part.

hallway that led through the cafeteria over to the library. The booing began as soon as they could see me and I could see them. Not everyone, but it sure felt like it. Getting from one end of the hallway to the other seemed to last a lifetime.

The next day a boy who claimed to like me, but booed along with everyone else, came to apologize on behalf of the other kids in his class. How embarrassing. The onlooker apology would make a repeat appearance later in my life (I will explain more in Part II).

Later that year the morning pledge of allegiance was what would finally get the attention of the adults in my school. In the classroom the desks were arranged in two layer of a U shape - a smaller U in front and a larger U behind. I was standing at my desk located on the front row and directly behind me was a "mean girl" who enjoyed picking on me.

She thought she was so cool because she had long hair and hung out with the "cool" girl.

After the pledge of allegiance was over, the "mean girl" leaned over and stuck a pencil in my chair right before I sat down. I didn't know what was going on. As I took my seat I felt it, the pain of something in me. I jumped up and asked to go to the bathroom. I was in pain but I wasn't sure why. I heard laughter. When I got to the door, a friend of mine said, "Raushawna, something is sticking out of your butt.". I reached down, pulled the #2 pencil out of me, and ran to the nurse's office.

The nurse checked me out and called my Mom. She took me to the doctor where they checked my private area only to find I had a puncture wound half an inch from my vagina. Two stitches, one week of sitting on ice with a pillow, and no dancing were enough to make me consider ending it all.

One day after school I sat at my desk in my room and wrote a short note to my parents that said something like "I love you and school is way too hard. I don't

> I don't want to do *this* anymore.

want to do this anymore." Then I listened to Mariah Carey's "Hero" on my walkman (yes, I am old), tore up the note and cried until my mom called me down for dinner. I faked being okay that night, and figured if I could fake it then maybe no one would notice me faking it at school. I mustered up the courage to go back and tried to avoid the mean girls and focus on the friends I did have. They were and still are a Godsend. I didn't know God then like I do now, but I knew when I was writing that little letter and listening to Mariah that I was too scared to try something because I hadn't quite figured out death and what happened after.

If you or someone you know is in a dark place or is experiencing suicidal thoughts, reach out and get help. If you feel embarrassed or ashamed it is okay. Know you are not alone. Every day is a new day and there is so much more to living.
Visit www.suicidepreventionlifeline.org or call 1-800-273-8255 for more information.

I decided I would take it one day at a time. Get up, get dressed, go to school and LOVE the weekend. That worked!

I made it through elementary school and middle school is where I decided I would reinvent myself. Our middle school was bigger; three elementary schools all came together to form the graduating class of 1999. I discovered a bigger chorus, and realized a love for singing and show choir to go along with my dancing. This saved me. I could be me and no one cared because everyone was trying to find their way in middle school. I also learned, in order to sing classical music correctly, you had to enunciate. All of the things I was mocked for in elementary school were now gifts and assets I could use to create music! Sweet! I thrived in middle and high school by being me, the version of me that I liked.

I ran track, liked a few boys, and of course every now and again I was questioned about my "whiteness" and "blackness". When it came to that, I couldn't win! Being too white seemed to be an issue and being not black enough was also a perception many people held about me. I decided I would be me and that was enough.

I still remember feeling like I didn't care. I am going to be me and that is all I can be. I wasn't good at faking it and it was exhausting trying.

It was years later that I would reconcile in my mind how significant my elementary school

> "We do not learn from experiences...we learn from reflecting on experience."
> - John Dewey

experiences would be on my life. How profound the moments were in shaping what I believed about myself and what I was capable of achieving, even though from the outside looking in it appeared I was doing well and accomplishing so much.

I sang, danced, and played an instrument in public often and would even speak, off the top of my head, in public; but reading in public was still a challenge I faced. Until one day, I was thrust into a moment where reading in public meant housing for my fellow classmates and friends. On the campus of North Carolina A&T is where I finally put the fear of reading in public on trial and pronounced it a LIAR.

I read the names of hundreds of students waiting for notification about their room assignments. To this day I don't even remember how I ended up being the one with the list but there I was scared to read but ready to lead, so I did it. Some names I pronounced incorrectly and got looks and lots of corrections, but I did it. That is when I learned: doing it is better than wondering if I can and getting it right is not always the most important thing. Sometimes just doing it is enough to trick my heart and brain into believing in me and perhaps the same is true for you. Maybe we know deep down inside we can, but we need to get going and see our own progress to believe.

> That is when I learned: doing it is better than wondering if I can and getting it is not always the most important thing.

Sometimes, I imagine that the small voice inside of me is actually behind my right ear, like a bug on a windshield. That voice usually tells me I am not enough and I can't do something (even now as I write this). The more momentum I build up the harder it is for the voice to hold on. When I take off, it has no choice but to fly off and be gone. We have to get going and move fast enough so it has no choice but to let go.

As far as the booing and the pencil incidents, before embarking on writing this book, I hadn't thought about them in years. I knew then that half the people who booed did it because everyone else was doing it and they were followers. The ones who started it booed because they saw something in me that I had not yet seen in myself. I forgave "pencil girl" in middle school and we are even Facebook friends today.

I don't share these stores for pity, but rather to let you know they taught me something.

> Bullies recognize more about us than we do.

They taught me how to look for and recognize the patterns in my life. I studied Engineering in college which taught me how to recognize patterns and behavior to create systems and processes. I did what any Engineer would do. I looked for the patterns of repeated error and developed the process to overcome the error. In this case, teach the heart and mind how to recognize the pattern early and create a process response before the error occurs. In non-engineering terms, I figured out why this was happening to me and now I want to share it with you. There is a pattern to behavior that impacts us all if we let it. I figured it out. There is a code to crack when we face adversity and bullies. To put it simply, bullies recognize more about us than we do of ourselves.

They know we are Awesome, we just don't know it, yet.

Discover Reflection Questions:

1. Have you ever encountered a bully?
2. What do/did you tell yourself about the situation?
3. Take a few minutes to reflect on the story in your head and what your bullies might know about who you are?

Chapter 3 – Awesomeness is YOU!

Simple to say, but hard to believe until you have encountered the truth about who you are.

WHEN YOU KNOW that you know that you know, then you know, you know? Ever heard that saying? I have. It implies the understanding that a check and double check are necessary. I don't think that is true about knowing who you are and what you want out of life. This is where knowing your Awesomeness starts. It is the still, small voice or a lingering thought that lives inside of you. It is in your likes and dislikes and in what you find funny and what is not. It is in how you order food at a restaurant, pay a compliment to a stranger and hug a friend. It is in every game you play, conversation you hold, and life you touch whether you know it or not.

I started seeing my Awesomeness through the eyes of others, first. I couldn't recognize it, but others could and would share their thoughts with me. For instance, one day I got a phone call from a friend and she had a wonderful job opportunity, but she was nervous and cautious about taking it because it would mean moving and being away from her family. She wanted the job because it was something that could help her progress

> I asked questions to help her think *into* her answers.

in her career. However, she knew it might send her away too long and keep her from being with her family during the special life moments. It was a tough decision and so she called me, we talked on the phone for about 45 minutes. I didn't tell her what to do or what to think. I asked question to help her think into her answer, an answer that would be hers and that she would give to herself. I was coaching her and I didn't even know it. The 45 minutes seemed to rush by. Even better, they flew by for her too and she said that she felt so much better. Then she gave me an amazing gift: "Thank you, Raushawna, you are really good at this. I think this is your calling." Wow! My calling! Those words stayed with me and I held on tight to them. In that moment I did what most people would do, and said, "Oh you are so welcome, I am glad I could help you."

Here is what I learned: my Awesomeness is inside of me. It is waiting for me to wake it up, bring it out, and give it the life that will make me truly happy and help the world around me. My Awesomeness is helping others be their best. It's not because I want to be the only Giver of Awesomeness. We are all Givers of Awesomeness, if we choose to be.

Understanding your Awesomeness is about understanding how you are and who you are. It is you. Some days it doesn't feel as awesome as it should, but it is still there. Other days the Awesomeness is bursting out of you. When you tap into your inner self it is experienced by every sense in your body. More importantly, it connects with the senses of others you encounter on their life journey.

So how do you discover and identify your Awesomeness? It can be an external or internal discovery. Both are necessary to fully bring your Awesomeness out. It will prepare you to be ready to give it to others. It does not matter where you start and each person will start in a different place.

> Your perspective matters.

EXTERNAL DISCOVERY

The external discovery begins with your eyes and ears. It starts with the way you see the world around you. Your perspective matters. For instance, when you drive down the highway do you focus on the other cars around you or your destination? Can you recall any of the makes and models that were beside you? Do you recall the driver who was yawning as you passed? Shift your vision to the buildings and billboards. Which ones do you remember? Which ones caught your eye? Which one did you read and whose words brought you to a feeling or emotion? How you see the world and allow it to speak to you is how you begin to tap into more of who you are.

God uses everything to speak to us, but we must be willing to listen. I realized this one day when I was running late to a reception; I really didn't want to attend but I felt obligated. As I was approaching the building there was a sign on the walkway that read "Dream BIG". There was a girl in white clothing looking and reaching up to a white light. It was beautiful and it spoke to me. I laughed a little and said out loud, "okay I will." Then I went to the reception and from that moment forward I was excited to be there. I had a purpose for being there. The reception had a bigger purpose than my obligation. I heard a message about not giving up on dreams and I believe this book was written because of that small but profound message.

These moments when God speaks aren't always big and grand, but they are there. I guess it depends on who you are. It may not take that much for me to listen and it may take you more, but listen anyway and see the connections because they are there.

Think about people who survive serious car accidents, storms, and other life events. Often you hear people speak about their life flashing before their eyes or feeling a new sense of purpose about their life. That new-found purpose is probably from the understanding that life is short so why not give all that you have to each moment. Be awesome and look for your Awesomeness in the compliments you receive.

Another way God speaks to us is through affirmations from others. What are people saying to you about you? How have people seen you in their lives?

About two months into posting articles online, I received a compliment from a communications professional: "You are a great writer. You have a wonderful voice" (writer speak for saying something with words). I felt like a million bucks! I used to say, "I am not a writer. I am a terrible speller." What I realized is those two things are not the same. I can be an awesome writer and I can be a terrible speller which is why I have editors and people who give me candid feedback. I was holding myself back from moving forward because of my limiting beliefs about myself. I can be both a great writer and a terrible speller while still positively impacting the world around me.

Think back to your drive to work. What were you thinking about? What thoughts came to you that helped you create the PowerPoint for a meeting, remember the handouts for the call, or the birthday of your co-worker? What thoughts held you back from putting those ideas on the slides, using the handouts, and giving the card? Was it an external or internal thought?

Sometimes our internal thinking is what leads us towards or away from giving, helping, and contributing. The best part about knowing how and who we are is that we can give what we have and feel good about it.

INTERNAL DISCOVERY

Thoughts come from the mind and the mind is extremely powerful.

> "...as man thinketh in his heart, so is he."
> (Proverbs 23:7, NIV),
> "If you think you can or think you can't, you are right."
> (Henry Ford)

These quotes are words of wisdom when it comes to knowing your Awesomeness. If you don't know when you are awesome and where your Awesomeness takes place, it is hard to achieve success. Satisfying success is not fleeting over time, marginalized, or diminished. It is success because you defined it. It lasts longer than the party music plays. It persists in the quiet and peaceful places within your soul. It may even push you towards quieter, where new goals or challenges are birthed. A satisfying success can stand alone and often requires alone time to truly be fulfilled.

Other times, the thought of success can be hard. It may cause you to spend prolonged periods of time thinking about what you are going to do next when you make a decision. It can be called analysis paralysis, or it may be the thoughts that create an overwhelming feeling.

> The spiral down thinking is what I refer to as "the swirl" and this type of thinking leads to stress and anxiety over the "what if."

I can remember being around someone who was very overwhelmed. They were thinking themselves into a knot over a decision to have a conversation with an employee

that was not performing \
let's call this person Sara| \
Dorothy was making erro \
money, and Sarah neede \
This may sound simple to \
conversation meant Doro \
worse yet, Dorothy may \
about these outcomes ov

... know, that it is okay to \
essential to progres \
Worrying abo \
facing the \
where \
Awe \
Y

I asked Sarah a series of \
swirled pattern of thinkin_ \
was willing to take to move forward. In the end, the
conversation was not as hard as it was made up to be and
Dorothy was appreciative to have information to become
better. Come to find out, Dorothy was fearful she was
making mistakes but didn't know which ones, or how to fix
them. The conversation was helpful and allowed both Sarah
and Dorothy to grow.

The greatest gift we can give
someone is the truth. This
offers others the opportunity to

> The greatest gift we can give someone is the truth.

let their head and heart connect, align, and prepare for
action.

There are times when one is ready and times when one is
not. This is when going inside and finding out what matters
most is extremely important. It will help you tell your head
that you are overthinking this and it is not hard. Perhaps it
is your heart that needs the peptalk. You are safe, you
might get hurt but you are strong enough to heal. Going
inside and telling your head and heart what it needs to

keep moving forward. This is

t the unknown is worse than knowing and
eal fear. Knowing when you are strong and
ou are weak allows you to truly discover your
omeness. It gives you power to think into your future.
ur heart and mind are tools to help you discover and will
guide you towards using all of your gifts.

Discover Reflection Questions:

1. When you are driving or riding in a car, what do you notice?
2. Think of the last billboard you read, what did it say and how did it make you feel?
3. What do you say to yourself when you first wakeup in the morning?
4. How do you express gratitude to yourself for a job well done?

Part II – Guard

Guard your gates. Stand watch and notice what is to come in and should remain out.

Chapter 4 – The Tarnish Effect

Rubbing off the tarnish is one thing,
finding out why it came is another.

YOU MAY BE feeling something in your belly by now. It is not the last meal you ate, but the awakening of you, your Awesomeness! It is that inner drive that is now pushing you to read, learn, and bring your Awesomeness out.

For instance, you may see pictures in your mind of people, places, and things you desire. Your heart may race when you think of a dream that has been deferred, until now. It is time to make sure that you give all you have to this one life.

When I started on the journey to understand some of the most hurtful parts of my life, I went back and worked my way forward through all of the times when I was hurt, shamed, and rejected. I wanted to understand all of the times I was crying, broken, and feeling alone. What purpose did they have in my life?

I didn't want to create victims and villains out of each scenario. I did want to see if I could find a pattern. Perhaps it is the "Arranger" (StrengthsFinder 2.0) in me that needed to find a pattern, or maybe the Engineer in me that needed to crack the code, to make sure this didn't happen again. I wanted to understand if this behavior was my fault, and if so, how I could prevent it. How could I be different?

I wanted to understand how this happened to me. Was this my fault? Could I fix it? If I could fix it or at least tell my story then perhaps it would free someone else, someone like you, to know they are not alone and to shed light on the questions and possible answers I discovered.

I wanted to know how a person's demeanor in conversations could go from kind to mean in an instant. Why was respect and disrespect as easy for some people as shifting gears on a bike? Was I the only one who experienced these types of conversations as catastrophic tumbles off the proverbial cliff? I felt like I needed to know and understand all of the moments I faced that led me to ask, "how did I get here and by the way, I didn't sign up for this!?"

> What I noticed was "The Tarnish Effect" these moments had on my confidence and perhaps the same is true for you.

The tarnish of our Awesomeness is like silver in the china cabinet, hutch, or butler's pantry in a home. Even the best silver will tarnish if not stored and cared for properly. It happens slowly and over time. At first it is subtle and faint, hard to see until the tarnish takes over and you see the browns, purples, and blues start to creep in. The only way to get the tarnish off is to polish the silver (rub it off). The tarnish takes time to come and polishing it away is a slow pastime.

Sterling silver that is exposed to air will tarnish. It is the air that makes this chemical reaction occur. If you use the silver you have to take care of it to make sure that it stays bright and shining. The same is true of our gifts and talents and your Awesomeness. It must be well taken care of or it will tarnish.

If sterling silver is in an area with high humidity or where the air is polluted it will tarnish faster. The same is true for you and me. Think about who is around you. What kind of energy do they give off? Are they people who pollute the atmosphere with negative thoughts and actions? Are there people in your life who tarnish you?

> Are their people in your life who cause you to tarnish?

They may be people who puff up when there is conflict or say mean things when they are under stress. Perhaps they are a close friend who is trying to keep you safe when you have a desire to dream big. They could be a parent, cousin, sister, or brother who is tarnishing your talent because they can only see you for who you were, not for who you are today with all of the changes you have made.

You used to be an addict but have been clean for years and somehow they can only see you for what you used to be. The tarnish, if not rubbed off, will change the look and feel of silver and other precious metals. Our tarnish, if it remains, could leave us looking at ourselves differently.

You may have to guard yourself by changing your environment, creating boundaries, or distancing yourself from certain types of people as you seek to guard all of you.

If you are unsure if this is you, then start to pay attention when you are around certain people, groups, or environments. Your intuition will speak to you through your head and your heart. It will have you uneasy, shifting in your seat, feeling like your chest is tight or your stomach aches. Our bodies can't lie to us when it comes to matters of the soul. It doesn't know how. We have to listen and make changes to guard the gifts we have.

When we are put in situations that give us an opportunity to learn more about who we are and what power and authority we have, we must choose to guard what is precious. Keep all of you safe and remember everyone is not ready for all of your Awesomeness. That is not your problem it is theirs. You can protect yourself by choosing to find new environments that promote growth and transparency. That doesn't mean you don't share, but you share knowing you have to protect your gifts from the words, circumstances, and situations of life. The best way to guard your Awesomeness is to know when you are in situations where you are helping and when you are working.

"Helping" is defined as "making it easier for (someone) to do something by offering one's service or resources" and working is defined as "activity involving mental or physical efforts done in order to achieve a purpose or result." (dictionary.com)

Helping situations is a great moment for your Awesomeness to come out, and it is often exactly what is needed to get the job done. Your presence is needed, therefore, all of you is invited (your Awesomeness too). It can get tricky especially when you find yourself in a situation at work. You will need to listen to know when the right time is to bring more of you out. Be strategic at first. You can prepare others to expect more from you as you bring more of your authentic self to each situation.

When people are working they may or may not be thinking and feeling. Many people are working in organizations, but they aren't thinking. They are simply going through the motions of rote memorization or they are waiting for permission to be told what to do. They may not even have passion for what they do and they may expect you to be the same way. This is when guarding your gifts and talents are critical to ensuring you act based on your values and beliefs, not the environment in which you find yourself.

> I needed room, space, and freedom to create, fail, and try again.

You may find you can't thrive in this type of environment. This was true for me. I needed room, space, and freedom to create, fail, and try again.

I found this out the hard way. I used to work in an environment that was stuck. That's how I described it. "We've always done it this way," was the rote answer when new ideas or possibilities were discussed. It was considered a good, stable job and this thinking ruled many of my colleagues' behavior. "Don't rock the boat" was often said in meetings when it was time to make a critical decision.

I quickly found myself coming up against barriers and challenges, not because the work was hard, but because being in the box was safe and I represented risk and change.

I learned that I love to think outside of the box. Why do we even need a box? Could we have a sphere, a pentagon? Perhaps a cylinder or actually, an open space is just fine. The status quo culture was killing my soul daily. With a bullying boss and disjointed values (keep reading I will tell you more) I made a choice. I resigned and chose to venture out and explore all that God had for me. I wondered how far I could go and what I would learn.

That decision was the best. It allowed me to continue exploring my past, present, and what I believed God wanted for my future. This exploration led me to people from whom I had to guard my gifts. Soon I figured out there were people throughout my life who saw my Awesomeness and wanted to steal it. These people and situations were my greatest teachers and propelled me to believe in myself more.

Guard Reflection Questions:

1. What types of environments do you thrive in?
2. Which of your gifts or talents stands out to you?
3. How do you desire to use this Awesomeness in your life to positively impact others?

Chapter 5 –Stealers

Shine bright in the midst of darkness for it is there where
your light is needed most.

AWESOMENESS STEALERS ARE all around us. They are
preservationists at heart, and not for the sack of scrapbooks
and photo albums, but because it is familiar and they have
some sense of power and control over what they know.
They tend to be people that want to preserve the current
state of things, the tradition, the color, the pattern, the
process and their ideas. They don't even know they are
stealing our gifts and talents, but we know something is not
quite right.

These stealers learn to play
it safe, or better yet, they
have learned that the only
way to get what they want

> Stealers get something out of
> you staying exactly the way
> you are.

and need is by doing it themselves or repeating the same
thing over and over again. Stealers get something out of
you staying exactly the way you are.

This is the version of you they can recognize, understand, and control. Stealers tend to operate under the thinking "no one did it for me so I can't or won't do it for you." Just by being you, you can make an unsuspected stealer, nervous.

"I don't know what box to put you in. You have too many talents." I remember thinking WOW! I didn't

> "I don't know what box to put you in, you have too many talents."

understand I needed to fit into a box. I think I prefer a trapezoid if I am picking geometric shapes!

You can't share your gifts with everyone. Some only come to learn and look for an opportunity to label and take. You will be the giver and they the taker.

It could be that you have been in a relationship so long that you don't really notice the diminishing of your Awesomeness. You want to be married and your partner does not. They keep saying it is not the right time and you are left wondering will the right time ever come.

Maybe you are waiting to buy your first home and you keep waiting because your friends say your apartment is so cool and they love your pool, and enjoy coming over and hanging out with you. You stay so they have a place to come. You secretly wonder if you and your house are enough to keep these "friends".

You are more than enough, with or without the marriage, the house, or the things you've been waiting for to make you right or ready. There is no right, **there is you**. You have so much Awesomeness inside to give to others, so start exploring more of who you are and who you have been in your past. Look for patterns and behaviors in people you have encountered. If you are unsure who these people are, enter this process with me to learn how to guard against the five different types of behaviors that I've encountered and have come to identify as bully characters. Their behaviors steal our Awesomeness. They also leave us a wonderful trails of breadcrumbs to help us discover who we are meant to be.

<u>Guard Reflection Questions:</u>

1. What is one thing you want to accomplish that you are waiting on?
2. If you accomplished "it," how would your actions positively impact others?
3. Make a list of unsuspecting stealers that came to your mind when reading this chapter?

Chapter 6 – Deceiver

The truth is more than enough to
wage war on an enemy of the soul.

DECEIVERS ARE THE first type of Stealer I want to share
with you. Deceivers are people that take information that
you have and make you think that they're helping you when
in fact they are helping themselves. They deceive you into
thinking that you are the one that's getting more out of the
deal than they are. They are holding information you need
to do your job well and produce better outcomes quickly.

One time, I was asked to contribute and "outline a meeting"
I thought I would attend. I did the outline and filled in
specific details of what each section would cover with
questions to consider and more.

I learned later that the event was being conducted with
other people. Not only were the outline and details I put

together used, but they were presented as someone else's original ideas. I remember feeling taken aback that someone would do such a thing, that someone would ask me to do one thing for the purpose and use it for something very different.

> Not only were the outline and details I put together used, but they were presented as someone else's original ideas.

It may sound naive but I trust until I have a reason not to. I want to live my life open to people and the goodness they bring. However, I learned after this situation to ask more questions when working on projects and to not trust this specific person so much because they were a deceiver.

One situation to be cautious of with a Deceiver is when "collaboration" is occurring. I describe collaboration by using a meal analogy. If you and I come together and we're both hungry, we will collaborate to decide what we're going to eat. We may want to make lunch; we may decide, who cares we're making breakfast! We want pancakes, eggs, and bacon. Once we decide on breakfast we then get into teamwork and divide up what needs to be cooked and in what order. We share a common goal, which is to eat! The tasks get complete and goal accomplished - Full Bellies!

Effective collaboration requires you to know and trust the intentions of the person brought together to collaborate. Trust is foundational.

When I was working on that project I didn't have all of the information. I didn't understand there were more people joining the meal. I found that out through the course of working on the project. I began to recognize that I was not being told the full truth. There were pieces and parts of the work that were being held back and often times I would ask questions only to be met with frustration and anger. Occasionally, the Deceiver would question my ability or willingness to do the work. This was my sign that I had met my Deceiver.

> A Deceiver intentionally holds back information
> as a way to control you.

Perhaps you have met a Deceiver too. When it is all truth and out in the open, there is no need for unwarranted frustration. The most confidential matters can be met with kindness and honesty that some information cannot be shared. We can all understand these situations. The intention behind Deceiver behavior is laced with power and control.

This Deceiver behavior can be overcome and avoided. It requires us to first be aware that it is happening. You are not crazy, we are not crazy, even though the behavior and encounters can make us feel that way.

Once you are aware that this is happening you can choose to put boundaries or barriers around what the relationship is and when information is and is not shared. You can also understand how your role is related to the overall goal of the project and do your part and nothing more. You can also have a conversation to make the person aware that perhaps they are operating in this Deceiver behavior. Give them an opportunity to change.

I have to be honest during this time I did not have the confidence I do now so I didn't have the conversation. I didn't feel brave enough at the time to say what I wanted to say and I

> I was being taken advantage of and I allowed it.

wasn't really sure of the words that I wanted to use. I didn't want to face the uncomfortable truth. *I was being taken advantage of and I allowed it.*

All I wanted to do was race forward with my new truth. I began to look around. I began to notice and the more aware I became, the less I needed to say something; instead I began to do what I knew to be right. I wanted to take my gifts, talents, and power elsewhere. My Awesomeness was not safe there anymore and I knew it. I made a choice to value myself and you can too.

Choose you, and change. Once you change, you signal to everyone and everything around you that life is different. Sometimes the best conversations are the ones that are never had but mean the most. When I stopped giving my Deceiver access, I knew I was free. Deceivers can only thrive off of the information and energy you give. Go and give your Awesomeness to someone and focus on something else that needs and values you!

Be sure to guard and protect your Awesomeness, no matter what. You want to keep every ounce of confidence in yourself. Do not shrink back but walk with boldness and let your Awesomeness shine.

Guard Reflection Questions:

1. Have you encountered a deceiver?
2. What did they say or do that let you know you were not getting all of the information?
3. Now that you recognize some Deceiver behavior, what will you do?
4. How do you express gratitude to yourself for a job well done?

Chapter 7 – Hoarder

You cannot keep someone
who does not want to be kept.

AWESOMENESS HOARDERS ARE people who see your value and want to keep it for themselves. They may intentionally make you feel bad about wanting to move forward or beyond the constraints of your relationship with them.

They want to hide you from others. They don't introduce you to people, they find ways to hold you back or keep you in a small box. When you are around, they may try to intimidate you or make you feel scared to speak up and stand out.

> A Hoarder tries to keep you close. They don't want anyone else to have your gifts and talents.

Hoarders can think they are doing you a favor by not sharing you with others. From friends to managers to clients, the Hoarders behavior can feel like bullying if we don't recognize it for what it is: an understanding that you have a gift and they want it.

I noticed this pattern early on in my life. When I was in elementary school I was on the playground with my friend when a new girl asked to play with us. My friend said, "no, we can't play with her, you're my friend."

How many of you have had that moment?

Perhaps even today you have a friend that says you're "my friend" and doesn't like to share you with others.

When someone else needs a friend, a Hoarder wants to keep you away from them. They may say "you can't talk to them because you talk to me" or they get upset if you go to lunch, shopping, or just spend time with someone else. Hoarders tend to be jealous or possessive.

Hoarders may not know they are holding you back or limiting you. They may confess their love for you, but their love may feel conditional and hinders your ability to give more of your gifts and talents to others.

The hoarders that have been in my life from playground to adulthood have always loved me so much so they wanted to keep me close. I started to

> I started to feel like my options were limited, which made me resentful.

feel like my options were limited, which made me resentful.

I noticed this behavior at work as well. Managers would intentionally hold back their team members from applying for positions because they didn't want to lose their talent. They would tell them, "I can't afford to lose you."

I also started noticing this behavior was contagious. I found myself holding back resources and giving opportunities to other people because I didn't want them to have a leg up on me. I didn't want to share.

This is when I knew I had a problem and needed to make a change. I am naturally a giver. If you find yourself in a relationship where you are doing things that are counterintuitive to who you are naturally, then perhaps you have encountered a hoarder and their behavior is rubbing off on you.

You have to recognize this behavior as a problem in order to fix it. You have to acknowledge you are in an unhealthy situation and need to make a choice. This choice does not need to be publicly announced or posted on a social media,

> You have to recognize this behavior as a problem in order to fix it.

but rather, it is an awakening. A moment within where we tell ourselves to set boundaries. It's an epiphany.

Some people will honor your shift and become more aware. Others will feel rejected or abandoned and experience a sense of loss. There may even be stages of grief, such as anger or denial that is left behind. If the relationship is worth sustaining, it must be renegotiated to ensure you don't fall back into the Hoarder's tendencies. If left unattended, Hoarder behavior can lead to manipulation in a relationship which does more damage to you.

Remember to guard your Awesomeness. It is the primary reason the Hoarder behavior is impacting your life. They see your potential and want to do whatever they can to keep you close and under their control. Breakout and guard who you are.

Guard Reflection Questions:

1. Have you encountered a Hoarder?
2. What did they say or do that let you know they were trying to keep you to themselves?
3. Now that you recognize some Hoarder behavior, what will you do?

Chapter 8 – Minimizer

Be careful, small people may look tall on the outside, but the inside is where their heart lives.

THE MINIMIZERS THAT have been in my life have taught me the most. Minimizers get joy out of making us feel small.

The last time I saw an influential minimizer in my life I was standing with a slight tilt of my head and I was taking in the picture of my minimizer who was standing proudly as they made me feel small in a public setting.

My Minimizer was my boss. In three months I went from confident and happy to anxious and ill. I was working out 3 to 4 days a week and eating semi-healthy, but my blood pressure was consistently above 140.

One day, after a meeting with my "bully boss", my blood pressure was 155 over 87. The vein in my neck was pushing so hard you could see it and I had a pounding headache.

I was sick from the inside, and to most people I seemed a little more stressed as we were "transitioning", but I knew differently. I knew this Minimizer was threatened and was trying to do everything they could to "put me in my

place." They would say things like:
- "I don't have time to meet with you."
- "Oh you think you're good don't you?"
- "This is what happens when you get ahead of yourself."
- "Look at me when I am talking to you."

When I last saw this Minimizer. I noticed the moment of joy on their face. They enjoyed making me feel small and I knew I had to make a change. I felt sick, my head and stomach ached. I called the doctor again and the next day I went in for an appointment.

A Minimizer gets joy out of making you feel small.

In the doctor's office is where the sum of it all washed over me as my doctor asked me questions about my recent medical history. Have you experienced:
- loose bowels
- uncontrollable bladder
- stomachaches
- headaches
- blurred vision

I answered yes to every question and the more I said yes, the more I cried. I couldn't believe this was who I had become in such a short amount of time. I did not know these symptoms were related to what I was experiencing at work. I thought this was my fault; I was getting older and this was all a part of it.

My doctor recommended I report this behavior. I didn't feel comfortable doing that, but I did take the doctor's advice and go out on leave to let my body heal.   After a couple of weeks my blood pressure was down and all of my other symptoms were gone.

My boss was killing me, not my job. I loved the work I did. It was challenging. I wasn't always right and I wasn't always wrong, but I was made to feel like I wasn't good enough.

> My boss was killing me, not my job.

That is what Minimizers do. They make you feel like what you do is never enough. You try to adjust to "feedback" and it still is not right. I was second guessing every decision and that was not me.

You know you have encountered a Minimizer if what used to seem so easy is now challenging and you feel small on the inside. When you leave this person's presence you may feel like the walls around you are closing in. Assess your feelings and begin to paying attention.

On page 16 I shared with you the example of the "onlooker apology". This is another way you know you have encountered a Minimizer. People who witness a Minimizer getting joy out of making you feel small will come and try to apologize on their behalf.

After my last encounter with my bully boss two colleuges came to me and tried to apologize for the way I was treated.

I quickly stopped them because while I believed their intentions were good, the behavior was inappropriate.

If you see such behavior and aren't willing to stand up and say something about it in that moment, then you give the Minimizer permission to continue the behavior. Sometimes onlookers say things like, "that's just how they are" or "they're having a bad day". This is a sign for you, a gift, that you are experiencing a Minimizer and you have a gift and talent they want!

Unlike Hoarders, Minimizers know exactly what they are doing and they like it. They are small inside and fearful that you have gifts and talents they don't. They see your Awesomeness and need to put you in your place. They may even let you shine, but they are going to make sure your light is not as bright as it could be.

After being out on leave for thirty days, I resigned. I am grateful to my Minimizer for coming. They taught me so much about who I am and what I have to offer. This is why it is important to study each Stealer characteristic. Each helps us unlock gifts and talents we possess.

Minimizers are people who see your talent and use it against you. When you do something that comes easy to you, they get angry, frustrated, or belittle you in private or public settings. It is as if they cannot control themselves because they can't do what you can and if they can, it does not come easy, and that bothers them. When you encounter a Minimizer and you see them getting joy out of making you small, know they see your Awesomeness and keep going!

Guard Reflection Questions:

1. Have you encountered a Minimizer?
2. What did they say or do that made you feel small?
3. Now that you recognize some Minimizer behavior, what will you do?

Chapter 9 – Penalizer

Hold back if you must, but never forget,
all that you withhold you will eventually loose.

PENALIZERS SEE YOUR Awesomeness and find ways to
punish you for just being you. They hold back emotions and
access as a way to get back at you for using your gifts and
talents.

The hardest part about trying to have a healthy relationship
with a Penalizer is that you could be in competition with a
Penalizer, not know it, and be winning. They are very
focused on what you are doing. They want to know what is
going on in your life, work, and business. They want to use
that information against you later.

I remember a time in my professional career when I was
praised for my innovation,
bravery, and courage. I had
people coming to me because
they valued those attributes. I

> They begin to punish
> you for the things they
> once admired most.

even had a team member publicly thank me for being a

champion for creating a new work culture, yet later, that same person ostracised me for being creative. They began to punish me for the things they once admired most.

Penalizers use tactics, such as the silent treatment, passive aggressive tones, and limiting your access to resources and information to let you know they are displeased with you. You may not even recognize it at first, because what got you in this position was you being you. However, the Penalizer in your life may be trying to tell you to slow down, or even STOP.

I often talk to adults who share their stories of Penalizer family members who use the silent treatment or short, one-word answers as a way of punishing them for choices they are making in their life.

Have you ever shared good news with family or friends only to meet a disappointing responses?

- "If that is what you want."
- "Okay"
- "You're going to leave me."
- "Do you."
- "Hi"
- "Bye"
- Silent treatment
- Eye rolling

A Penalizer holds back access and emotions as a way to punish you for your actions.

When my husband and I were going to move to California, so many people asked us how our parents would feel about our move. I remember one colleague said, "if I moved to California, my Mom wouldn't talk to me for weeks." This is a classic example of Penalizer behavior. A great opportunity can quickly turn into a "what have you done to me" conversation when Penalizer behavior shows up in your life. It can feel like you are being bullied into changing your mind.

When I was younger I had a friend who had a boyfriend I did not like. I thought he was a jerk. I didn't like the way he spoke to her and treated her around his friends. I just didn't like him. One day, she asked me what I thought about him and their relationship, so told her. I told her the truth. I shared with her examples of times I thought he was disrespectful and jerkish. We didn't talk for six months.

This is classic Penalizer behavior.

Your Penalizer may not be able to recognize the impact of their behavior. They may be reacting to an internal hurt or pain they have inside. They may not know how to process their feelings and instead of saying how they feel, they try to make you feel the way they feel. They hurt you. They punish you for your good actions and intentions.

You know you have encountered a Penalizer when your honesty, effort, success, idea or dreams now cause you pain and that pain is coming directly from another person or group.

This is when remembering your why is so important. Why did you want to share, go, be and do the thing you desire? Why are your ready now to take action and step out into what is next for you? Your *why* can combat any punishment a Penalizer tries to bring. You may even find that the punishment is a gift in disguise.

Your Awesomeness is directly tied to your ability to trust your own decision-making capabilities and be true to what you know and believe.

Release the Penalizer and let them sort out their feelings while you keep moving forward. They will either become your biggest fan or they won't. Either way, the choice is theirs. Do not allow this type of behavior to steal your joy and confidence.

Guard Reflection Questions:

1. Have you encountered a Penalizer?
2. What did they say or do that made you know they were withholding access and emotions from you?
3. Now that you recognized some Penalizer behavior, what will you do?

Chapter 10 – Taker

Hold on tight to the joy you have for it is worth more than any physical gift given.

THE LAST STEALER I will discuss is the Taker. A Taker infringes on moments of joy in your life and wants you to feel bad about something good. Takers are good at seeing your value and taking a little piece of it, moment by moment.

I experienced this when I was a senior in high school. I told a teacher in my building I was attending North Carolina A&T State University (Aggie Pride), she said, "You would go there?" I remember the look on her face. She questioned my choice because she didn't think I was Black enough to go there.

My high school was predominantly White and there were very few Black students. I was one of a few Black girls who wasn't on the step team. This teacher did not know me well, but I believe, based on their tone, they had a bias about who I was and where I should or would choose to go to college.

NC A&T is a Historically Black College and is one of the largest producers of Black Engineers in the United States. It was the perfect choice for me because I wanted to study Engineering. I wanted to have a different college experience than my K-12 education. This teacher did not know that about me and in the moment tried to make me feel bad about my choice.

I remember being much more cautious about who I shared my future plans with as the year came to an end. I would hear statements like, "you are studying what" or "where is your college."

> Takers can turn a moment of joy and celebration into embarrassment and shame because of their preconceived ideas or misplaced expectations.

We have to guard our Awesomeness and know how to stand firmly and securely in these moments. We have to be willing to make the choice anyway and move forward with confidence.

Have you ever had an idea that you shared with a close friend or family member only to be met with:

- "Are you sure you want to do that?"
- "You might not make any money."
- "What is that - I don't get it?"
- "Don't ask me for help."

Whatever they comment, they didn't lift you up but rather made you feel bad about something good.

Perhaps you did accomplish something, a moment of completion or success:

- "You think you're hot stuff."
- "You weren't that good."
- "I bet you can't do that again."

- "You always get recognized."
- "How come you didn't invite me?"
- "Why didn't you tell me first?"

> A Taker infringes on moments of joy in your life and wants you to feel bad about something good.

These are all Taker comments. The comment is infringing on your ability to enjoy the moment of joy. Takers are people who see you, your gifts, your Awesomeness, and they want to steal it. They want to suck the joy and life right out of every idea, dream, or word you say. They are always your "devil's advocate", ready to be the nay-sayer when all you need is a yay-sayer. These are people who get something out of you staying exactly the way you are. They are unable to see the change and growth in your life.

Be ready to put your Takers in their place, off to the sidelines, as you take your place on the field of life, doing what you do best! You don't have to feel bad about it, you have to give it all you have because your Awesomeness is worth it!

Guard Reflection Questions:

1. Have you encountered a Taker?
2. What did they say or do that diminished a moment in your life?
3. Now that you recognize some Taker behavior, what will you do?

Part III – Give

Give all that you have to good causes and people.

Chapter 11 – Attitude and Emotion

*It may be simple to say,
but that does not make it easy to do.*

WHAT IS THE difference between attitude and emotion? Attitude is defined as "manner, disposition, feeling, position, etc., with regard to a person or thing; tendency or orientation, especially of the mind." Emotion is defined as an "affective state of consciousness in which joy, sorrow, fear, hate, or the like, is experienced... and usually accompanied by certain physiological changes..."

The definitions are good and help define the words from a general perspective, however, I needed to define them for myself.

I started to think about what attitude and emotion meant to me, and the more I thought about it, the more I realized they are connected. Attitude is in the mind. It comes across in my words, non-verbal cues like eye rolls, hand gestures and more. All of these actions start with my thoughts and usually have an outward expression. My mind is where my attitude is birthed and leads me to think positive or negative thoughts about circumstances and situations. These thoughts either connect or withdraw me from people, places and things in my life. If my attitude is right, I feel like I can do anything. If my attitude is wrong, it's a long hard day. This is where the intersection with emotion begins.

Emotion is in the heart. What my mind says, my heart feels. If I think love, I feel love. If I think hate, I feel hate. It is what I give and receive from the world around me. I often encounter people who describe themselves as "emotional." I don't think that is a bad thing. In sports, emotion is shown as passion. Take Serena Williams as an example. She won the Australian Open and her 23rd Grand Slam. She is an emotional person, but she is also a person that has spent countless hours focusing on thinking positive thoughts. She and many other premier athletes think, "win" and so they win.

I want to win in my life, too. I want to be successful in the ways that matter to me. I choose to think and feel in the ways that bring me joy, that push me to be greater today

> I want to be successful in the ways that matter to me.

than I was yesterday. This is where my choice to be awesome shows up. On the days when I get it wrong, I learn something new and move on to tomorrow where I know I can get it right. I don't dwell in frustration. I ask myself questions that help me to move past frustration into action.

Taking action and trying again is where attitude and emotion create the Awesomeness that is necessary to lead a fulfilling life. I think it is important to define what you want for your life. Not what others want for you, not the American Dream from your parents, but what will make you feel like your life has meaning and purpose. In that reflection and definition you will find your Awesomeness. You can figure out the type of attitude and emotion you need to have to achieve the life you want.

In the end I realize attitude and emotion go together. Sometimes I think they take turns leading and it is up to me to decide which one is best suited to lead in what situation. Both exist to help me be a Giver of Awesomeness.

Making the choice around the type of attitude you will have in a situation can be the deciding factor between getting what you want or not. It can be what draws awesome people to you or keeps them from coming into your life and giving you the resources you need.

> The wonder is what makes it special.

Sharing your Awesomeness with others is a choice too. If you choose to share, the possibilities are endless. Endless possibilities are like rocks you drop in the water that create ripples as far as the eye can see. Choosing to share your Awesomeness is just like that. You never really know how far it goes. The wonder is what makes it special. On the contrary, if you choose not to share your Awesomeness then it is yours and it is safe. You will always know where it is, on the shelf of your heart, like a collectors item. It is there to be looked at and adorned by you and you only. It has value and is valuable however you may not know just how valuable until you take it off the shelf and let others see it.

Did you know some collectors have items that they have kept for years, only to find out they have very little value, or better yet, the item they have kept for so long is worth a life's fortune or more. Until they share their item with others, they may not know just how valuable it is. The same is true for you and your Awesomeness. It has value and is valuable. No one will deny that or take it from you, but when you share it with others its value goes on and on because others get to experience it over and over and give it to others. Then it becomes priceless.

I learned to choose to give and be all-in in my relationships. I remember the conversation I had with my Dad about my boyfriend when I was in college. My Dad was concerned because "I love him Dad, I really do" came right out of my mouth after knowing him for three months. My Dad did not want me to get hurt and "put all my eggs in one basket." I had just turned 20 years old, and although we had only been dating three months I knew he was the one for me. I told my Dad "I am going to give this relationship my all and if it doesn't work it won't be because I didn't try my best." I still remember his voice on the phone, calm but stern, "well all right then."

I knew something my Dad didn't know, I could and would honor my choice, no matter the outcome.

This is what bringing all of yourself means in any situation. It is where confidence is born. Confidence is the ability to believe and conduct ourselves accordingly, that whatever we encounter we are fully capable and equipped to handle the situation. It is about declaring that I can and will be ready for whatever comes. That day I chose love and daily I continue to make the same choice.

For you it could be commitment to a career, abstaining from sex or alcohol. No matter the choice, big or small, it is your choice and it is where your inner strength grows. Every time you make a choice you grow stronger. Awesomeness is not about these moments of grandeur, but it is how we choose to live out or life and it happens daily. Choose, decide, and declare. Life is much more fun that way!

<u>Give Reflection Questions:</u>

1. What type of attitude will you have today?
2. How do emotions affect your daily outcomes?
3. What is one change you desire about your attitude and emotion?
4. How do you express gratitude to yourself for a job well done?

Chapter 12 – Where To Be Awesome

Everywhere you go, be yourself.
Everyone else is taken.

NOW THAT YOU have found your Awesomeness or are well on your way to finding it, you absolutely want to know where to use it. The answer is simple: anywhere. Hopefully, everywhere you go. Awesomeness should be wherever you are, even in spaces and places where it seems like no one wants the real you to come out. When you get comfortable with being you, then you don't have to worry about being anyone or anything else.

One day I spoke at a women's empowerment event. After the event ended, a woman came up to my table and asked me a few questions. We talked and made a great connection. She said to me, "you are just as cool off the stage as you are on stage." I told her this is who I am and I don't know how to be anyone other than me. Her comment stayed with me because I knew she had experienced someone off stage who was very different than their on stage persona. It is a lot of work being someone else. I would much rather be me and I think that is where Awesomeness lives.

Think about when you were younger and learning how to ride a bike. As you got started, it was hard. Getting your feet on the pedals, looking up, going straight, and balancing seemed like more than you could do. You may have had a parent holding on to the back of your seat helping you. They were running with you to help you get the hang of it. Finding your Awesomeness is just like that, you have friends, family, colleagues, and more who are running beside you and wanting to help you find your gifts and talents. As you are searching, it may feel uncomfortable and at times like more than you can do, but keep trying, searching, and listening, because you will find a pattern in your life that lets you know you are on track. Once you find it, you will take off, going faster and further than you thought possible. Knowing that

> Hiding your gifts and talent is taught behavior.

you can be awesome anywhere and at any time will feel like riding a bike with your eyes closed, no hands and the wind in your face.

Hiding your gifts and talents is taught behavior. It is in how we are raised, what we learn in school or the organizations we join. It isn't even intentional. It is subtle and happens over time. Sometimes it is passed down generation to

generation. This undercurrent of don't outshine your _____
(fill in the blank with a family member) comes across in a
variety of ways.

Often times when you are around people that aren't sure
who they are and what their purpose is, it can feel
uncomfortable. They may have had harsh life experiences
that have led them to believe they are less and they cannot
achieve more. Therefore, when you are around and you
start speaking about what you are working on, it can bring
up hard feelings for them. Their smile dims, their head
drops, and their shoulders may round forward. These are
their personal feelings, they aren't your fault, but they can
leave you thinking and feeling like you did something wrong.

As a result, the next time you are with that person or in that
group, you share a little less and try to not share out of fear
that you will get a look or be ostracized for trying to have
more, be more, or do something different than what others
expect.

This is when you have to remember all you have learned
about the Stealers and bully characters. It could be that you
need to become aware of this behavior to guard your
Awesomeness.

Work

Awesomeness can be hard to share at work. Especially if
you work for and with others who haven't yet found their
gifts and talents. They may feel like they need to keep you
from being so great because it makes them uncomfortable.

Perhaps you have heard the statement "we've always done it this way" when presenting a new idea. This is code for, "don't bring your Awesomeness here. We aren't ready yet."

It does not mean they can't **get** ready but you may have to decide if this is the right place for you to grow.

> Can you endure holding back parts of you to preserve the comfort of others?

I remember when I was in charge of a three shift operation in a manufacturing plant. There was a team member, let's call him Ray, who was very talented. He was also very comfortable on third shift. I needed him to run a large project and that required him to move shifts and come to first shift. Most people who have worked on third shift understand that when a first shift (day shift) job comes open, you go for it. Not Ray. He wasn't sure he wanted to deal with the bosses and the daytime action, however, Ray trusted me enough to try.

He came to first shift, ran the project, and delivered outstanding results for the organization and himself. Ray ended up staying on first shift and today he is a still leading and making a difference for others.

I knew I had an ability to lead others before I worked with Ray, however, Ray became my personal evidence of what could happen for someone else when I listened to my instinct and was persistent in my pursuit of what I felt was right to elevate talented individuals.

Fast forward in my career to a new leadership position but the same heart for people. When I joined my new team I started assessing the roles and talent of each team member. What I quickly learned was that I had one person, let's call her Tiffany, who was overqualified and under-utilized in her current role. During my first meeting with Tiffany I asked "Are you currently looking for a new job? How much time do I have?" She looked at me in awe. Eyes wide, mouth open and then the icing on the cake, the nervous laugh. I knew I was on to something! I asked the question again, in a different way. "Are you leaving now, or do I have some time to fix this?" By the end of our first meeting I knew what I had to do. I asked Tiffany to give me some time and trust that I would be transparent with her throughout the process. If I couldn't make a change I would help her move on to a more fulfilling role, even if that meant off my team or out of the organization.

I believe great leaders make room for others. They teach them how to hone their gifts and talents and create room, space, and opportunities to lead. It is only through experience that some lessons can be learned and in leadership, creating experiences for others is a responsibility and honor.

In Tiffany's case, I was able to help her shift into a new role where she could operate in her sweet spot! It was a moment of joy when I told her the news.

For many, this concept is unknown or unwanted. The "no one did it for me so I will not do it for them" mentality plagues managers. John C. Maxwell says "People do what people see" and he calls this the Law of the Picture in "The 21 Irrefutable Laws of Leadership." This is why you have to be willing to bring all of you to your role at work. You may be the only person that can contribute to changing the picture of leadership.

If the picture of leadership is laced with self-preservation and do as I say - not as I do thinking, then an organization can quickly find they have a large number of managers that reproduce mediocrity.

It becomes ingrained in the culture of the organization. The culture is to hide, to play small and safe, and to leave most of what makes you awesome at the door. Sometimes it sounds like, "it makes us look bad." Your Awesomeness can't make someone else's awesome look bad. It can only enhance it. Each person has to be willing to bring and share their Awesomeness with others. This is the true meaning of being a Giver of Awesomeness.

Home

That old saying, "home is where the heart is", should have another part which is that "home is where your awesomeness roams free." Take laundry for an example. Laundry to me is like the Neverending Story. It goes on and on. Unless you are a practicing nudist, each day there are clothes that get dirty and have to be washed.

> The secret to success is in the small moments that impact life in profound ways.

It is important to know who has what Awesomeness when it comes to laundry. In my house, my husband's Awesomeness comes in as a saving grace in this and other areas. He usually starts laundry and I fold it and put it away. He tries very hard to fold, but his skills are less than desirable. I don't like the sorting and putting it in the machine. We both work in our areas of strength and no one gets overly frustrated by the household chore that won't end.

Same is true for cooking. He does most of the cooking. I do a lot of the eating! I can cook but he enjoys quiet time after a long day and cooking is fun for him. While the kids and I are out socializing and doing our thing he is cooking us a great meal and having his time. We both get what we need and want out of our life, and we do it together.

It may sound small but the secret to success is in the small moments that impact life in profound ways. You and I both know people who are bitter and waiting on someone else to do what they can do for themselves. Don't let yourself fall into that trap. Instead, be you and be awesome everywhere your feet are planted.

Beyond

I can't box you or me into thinking that work and home are the only places to be awesome. It sounds simple, but it is not easy. It takes courage and a conscious choice to bring your gifts out and have them met with the world and all of the different people out there.

There are many situations in our lives where bringing Awesomeness out will help others. You will be a person who adds value. It could be in your church, your community, in a group, on the playground or in the boardroom. No matter where you are, choosing to bring your Awesomeness with you and sharing it is a gift worth giving!

Give Reflection Questions:

1. How do you give your Awesomeness at work?
2. In what way do you give your Awesomeness at home? Work?
3. What is your heart's desire about where else you would like to share your Awesomeness?

Chapter 13 – Small Gifts Impact Lives

An act of kindness can give someone hope,
which can ignite flames of possibilities.

WHETHER YOU ARE a person of faith or not, there is a consistent principle of sowing and reaping. If you sow into others, you will reap what you sowed either through them or someone else.

Today, that is exactly how I try to see people. I try to give them more than what they are giving me. Some days I fall short, but most days I am able to give them something they need and in return I get what I need which is energy and love.

Think about who you are as sand at the beach. When you go to the beach sand is everywhere. In its ability to be sand, it has the possibility to get in every nook and cranny, and I mean everywhere! The same is true with your gifts and talents. They seep out of you no matter how hard you try to hold them back. Your spirit is energy and energy is transferred, not lost. To give the most to others and yourself, give all of you to areas where you will not be drained and can refill while seeing an impact in the lives of others. This is what being a giver of Awesomeness is all about.

> Everyday God gives us ways to give with the expectation that we will reap when the time is right.

I try to do a few things each week. I don't always get it right or remember but I try and that is an awesome start.

- Drink coffee? The next time you are waiting in line or in the drive thru, buy the person behind you a cup of coffee. This is an easy way to give and it can be known or unknown to the receive. Also, the ripple effect of your generosity is never known and that is what makes it awesome!

- Arguments? When you are in a conversation with someone who disagrees with your point and you can feel the conversation turning into an argument, take a deep breath and tell them they are right. Not in a condescending way, but in a genuine, you can win this one tone. If the topic isn't life or death then more likely than not, the other person can win, and that is okay. You don't have to win to be right. You don't have to win to be better. Sometimes letting go is the best way to get what you really want. It's called progress.

- Delegate? This one can be tricky because sometimes delegation can be experienced as a leader giving a follower the work they don't want to or cannot do. If you want to show someone a deep level of respect, delegate to them the work you love. The receiver will know you trust them. Trust is built over time and requires opportunities to demonstrate trustworthiness. When you share all you have with others, you give them an opportunity and that is all someone may need to build their confidence.

- Let Go? Similar to delegation but this specifically applies to other people. Let people pursue their passions and dreams. Sometimes this means giving them room, space, and time to be all in with something other than you. It can be a colleague who gets a new job and is considering leaving. It could be a life partner who needs to travel more as they pursue a promotion. It could be a friend who isn't around as much because they are spending time practicing for their moment. Each of these situations require you to let go. As you let go, people will experience Awesomeness in you as a supporter and in themselves as a person who can achieve greatness.

- Fail? There is something exciting about failure. Think about it. When you see people trip, don't you laugh inside, at least a little? What about when you see someone get scared and they flap around and scream loudly and then come back and regain their composure? That is failure and it can be hilarious! It is the losing of our composure that we find our common human side and where Awesomeness lives. It is not in being perfect and all put together. It is in the acknowledgement that this didn't go right, and I will fix it and try again. It is in the understanding that today I burned the chicken and tomorrow it might be the roast, but it is fun doing life with you. It is in the moment where the pitch to the client was awful and you learned valuable lessons for the next time. The more you can accept your failures and help others move forward through their own, the more Awesomeness you give.

I could go on and give more examples, but these are a few that really stand out to me and they are what I do on a regular basis. Sometimes it is easy and other times I have to remember who God said I am and do it anyway. Either way, I make a choice to continue. I choose to believe I

> I choose to believe I have something to give to others and then I give it.

have something to give to others and then I give it. It doesn't matter if people grab hold or not. It's about my willingness to try.

If I can try, then so can you. We can all be a Giver of Awesomeness if we choose to take each moment and be brave and open to who we are. You have so many gifts and talents to give to the world around you. Keep looking within and challenging yourself to explore and discover more of you.

Once you find hidden gifts, be sure to guard them from stealers and bully characters that come along. They can see your Awesomeness and will use it for their purpose, if you let them. Stay empowered and give your Awesomeness to people, places, environments and ideas that align to your values and beliefs. No matter what happens, Be a Giver of Awesomeness!

For continued learning:

1. How will you give your Awesomeness today?
2. What gifts will you share with others?
3. What impact would you like to make on the community around you?
4. What talents are you ready to give to the word?
5. What does being a Giver of Awesomeness mean to you?

Join the "Giver of Awesomeness Nation" group on Facebook to continue the discussion and ask questions to help you Discover, Guard, and Give your Awesomeness!

Visit giverofawesomeness.com for more information about workshop and resources.

Notes

1. New International Version of the Holy Bible, Proverbs 23:7.

2. Rath, Tom, StrengthsFinder 2.0, (Gallup Press, 2007), 53.

3. Dictonary.com, 2019

4. Maxwell, John C., The 21 Irrefutable Laws of Leadership, (Thomas Nelson, 2007), 155.

Acknowledgements

Thank you Lord for giving me this gift. Each word poured out is from you. Every experience in my life brought me to this moment to serve your people. I am humbled and grateful you chose me.

Jovani — Babe, "I love you" is not enough but it's what I've got. You are everything that is good and right in this world to me. You have been a solid humble rock as I have walked in obedience to God's will, even when it was crazy faith that got us through. May this be just the beginning of a new chapter in our story!

Zion and Zoe you two are my greatest gifts. I pray God honors your sacrifice with the desires of your heart. I am blessed to be your Mama and Mommy and I love you!

To my parents, Mom, Dad, Amee, and Pops I love you. Each of you has prayed for Jovani and I in your own special way. You have watched us transition our lives, from place to place, season after season. Through it all you've been there. Thank you for loving us as only parents can.

To my prayer warriors near and far, thank you for covering

me as I journeyed to an uncomfortable place to be obedient to the Lord. I am so glad he sent you into my life, for such a time as this. I love you.

To my "Village Queens", you know who you are. We've been through it all and have supported each other in the best and worst of what life brings. May this be one of the best times! I am the first who will be next?

To my bullies, Thank You! I could not have written this book without you. I am grateful for every breadcrumb you left to help me find my greatest gifts.

To my team and inner circle! Thank you for pushing me to finish this and not shrink back. Your belief in this work sustained me. Thank you for speaking my name and how this book blessed you, when it was being formed.

About the Author

Raushawna Price is an international leadership and success coach, speaker, and facilitator. She is also a real estate investor who enjoys funding deals for passionate entrepreneurs. She is a graduate of North Carolina A&T State University and Purdue University, where she earned a Bachelor and Master degree in Industrial and Systems Engineering, respectively. She also holds a Master of Educational Leadership from The Broad Center. Raushawna lives in Lake Wylie, South Carolina, with her awesome husband, Jovani, and their two children, Zion and Zoe. She enjoys working out and traveling!

Made in the USA
Columbia, SC
09 November 2019

82784276R00059